Jackie Robinson

A Photo-Illustrated Biography

by Barbara Knox

Consultant:
James L. Gates Jr., Library Director
National Baseball Hall of Fame and Museum, Inc.
Cooperstown, New York

Bridgestone Books
an imprint of Capstone Press
Mankato, Minnesota

Bridgestone Books are published by Capstone Press
151 Good Counsel Drive, P.O. Box 669, Mankato, Minnesota 56002
http://www.capstone-press.com

Library of Congress Cataloging-in-Publication Data
Knox, Barbara.
    Jackie Robinson/by Barbara Knox.
    p. cm—(A photo-illustrated biography)
    Summary: Examines the life of the talented black athlete who broke the color barrier in
major league baseball by joining the Brooklyn Dodgers in 1947.
    Includes bibliographical references and index.
    ISBN 0-7368-2224-0 (hardcover)
   1. Robinson, Jackie, 1919–1972—Juvenile literature. 2. Baseball players—United States—
Biography—Juvenile literature. 3. African American baseball players—Biography—Juvenile
literature. [1. Robinson, Jackie, 1919–1972. 2. Baseball players. 3. African Americans—
Biography.] I. Title. II Series: Photo-illustrated biographies.
GV865 .R6 K57 2004
796.357'092—dc21   2002156747

Editorial Credits
Christianne C. Jones, editor; Steve Christensen, series designer; Enoch Peterson,
    book designer and illustrator; Kelly Garvin, photo researcher; Karen Risch,
    product planning editor

Photo Credits
AP/Wide World Photos, 18
Corbis/Bettmann, 8, 16, 20
Getty Images/Hulton Archive, cover, 4, 6, 10, 12, 14

1 2 3 4 5 6 08 07 06 05 04 03

Table of Contents

"I know I am a black man in a white world. In 1972, in 1947, at my birth in 1919, I know I never had it made."
—Jackie Robinson, from his autobiography *I Never Had it Made*

Jackie Robinson

Jackie Robinson was the first person to break major league baseball's color barrier. The color barrier started in 1884. At that time, team owners agreed not to hire African American players. In 1947, Jackie played for the Brooklyn Dodgers. Many other African Americans played professional sports because of Jackie.

Jackie won many important awards. After his first season, Jackie was named Rookie of the Year. Two years later, he won the National League's Most Valuable Player (MVP) award. Jackie became one of the most famous baseball players of all time.

After his baseball years, Jackie helped fight for civil rights. He believed everyone should be treated the same. Jackie spoke at protests. He also gave money to many programs that helped African Americans.

Jackie Robinson broke major league baseball's color barrier.

Childhood

Jack (Jackie) Roosevelt Robinson was born January 31, 1919, on a farm near Cairo, Georgia. He was the youngest of Jerry and Mallie Robinson's five children. The Robinsons were sharecroppers. They rented farmland from a rich property owner.

Jackie's childhood was not easy. His father left the family when Jackie was a baby. His mother moved the family to Pasadena, California. The Robinsons were the only African American family on their block. Jackie's mother worked as a maid to support her family. She did not make much money.

Jackie went to school in Los Angeles. He loved to read and did well in school. Jackie also played sports. His best sports were track and field, football, basketball, and baseball.

Jackie (second from left) poses with his family for a portrait.

"Life is not a spectator sport. If you're going to spend your whole life in the grandstand just watching what goes on, in my opinion you're wasting your life."
—Jackie Robinson, 1964

College

After high school, Jackie went to Pasadena Junior College for two years. He led the football and baseball teams to championships. In track and field, he set a National Junior College record in the long jump.

In 1939, Jackie began to attend the University of California at Los Angeles (UCLA). He had been given a sports scholarship. Jackie played basketball, football, and baseball at the university. He was also on the track team. Jackie was UCLA's first athlete to win awards in four sports the same year. He also met his future wife, Rachel Isum, at the university.

But Jackie left UCLA in 1941. He did not finish college. Jackie needed to get a job and earn money to help his mother. He worked at a camp that helped children. Jackie also earned money playing semi-professional football.

Jackie participated in the long jump at many track meets for UCLA.

The Army

World War II (1941–1945) brought another change to Jackie's life. He was drafted into the U.S. Army in 1942. Jackie was sent to Fort Riley, Kansas, for training.

Jackie wanted to be an army officer. He applied to the Officer Candidate School. He was not accepted because he was African American. During WWII, African Americans were not allowed to be officers. But Jackie kept trying and was finally accepted into the school. He graduated and became a second lieutenant.

Even as an officer, Jackie faced problems in the army because of his race. The U.S. Army was still segregated during WWII. In 1944, an army bus driver ordered Jackie to move to the back of the bus because he was African American. Jackie refused to move. He was put on trial for refusing. At the end of the trial, Jackie was found innocent and released from the army.

Jackie became a second lieutenant after attending Officer Candidate School.

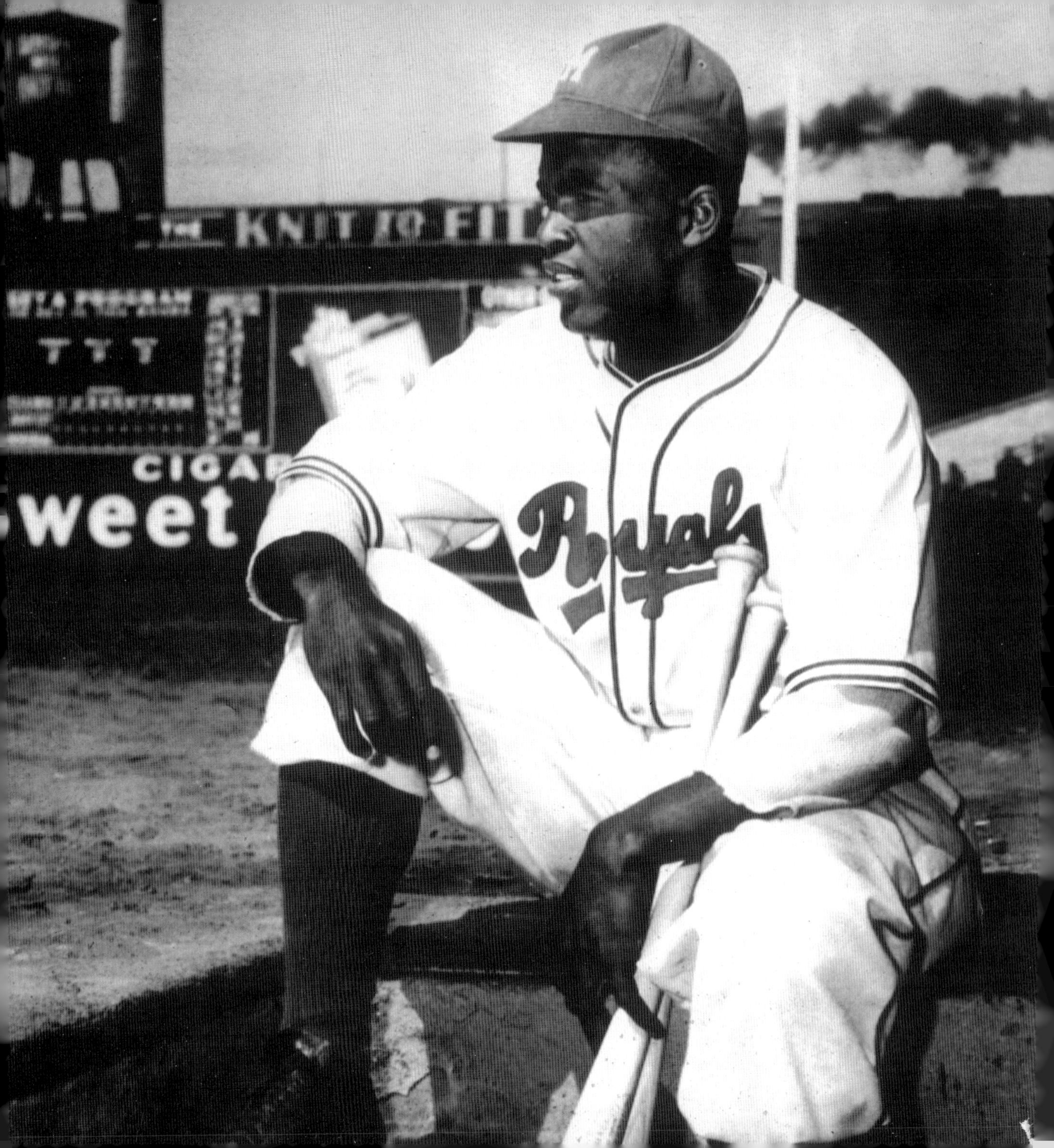
KNIT TO FIT
CIGA
weet
Royals

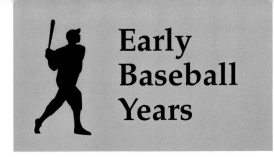

Early Baseball Years

After Jackie left the army, he decided to play baseball. He joined the Kansas City Monarchs in 1945. African Americans and whites still played in separate baseball leagues in the 1940s. The Monarchs were part of the Negro American League. This is where Jackie showed that he was a good hitter, runner, and fielder.

Branch Rickey saw Jackie's talent. Rickey was the owner of the Brooklyn Dodgers. He wanted Jackie to play for his team. Jackie had to promise that no matter how people treated him, he would not fight back.

Jackie signed with the Dodgers in 1945. He played his first season with the Montreal Royals. The Royals were the Dodgers' best minor league team. Major league teams often get players from minor league teams.

Jackie played one season for the Royals before playing for the Dodgers.

"I'm not concerned with your liking or disliking me...
All I ask is that you respect me as a human being."
—Jackie Robinson

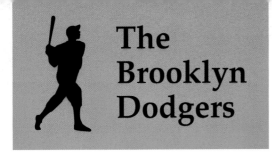

The Brooklyn Dodgers

After Jackie signed with the Dodgers, he married Rachel Isum. The wedding took place on February 10, 1946. The couple had three children, Jackie Jr., Sharon, and David.

After seeing Jackie's talent, the Dodgers wanted Jackie to play with their major league team. Jackie's first game with the Dodgers made history. On April 15, 1947, Jackie became the first African American to play major league baseball since 1884.

Many people did not want an African American to play on the team. Some fans shouted and threw trash at Jackie during games. Others held up hurtful signs or sent hateful mail to him.

Jackie did not fight back. Many people soon stopped treating him poorly. After a while, people began to respect Jackie and his talent.

Jackie started as the Dodgers' first baseman. He also played second base for the Dodgers.

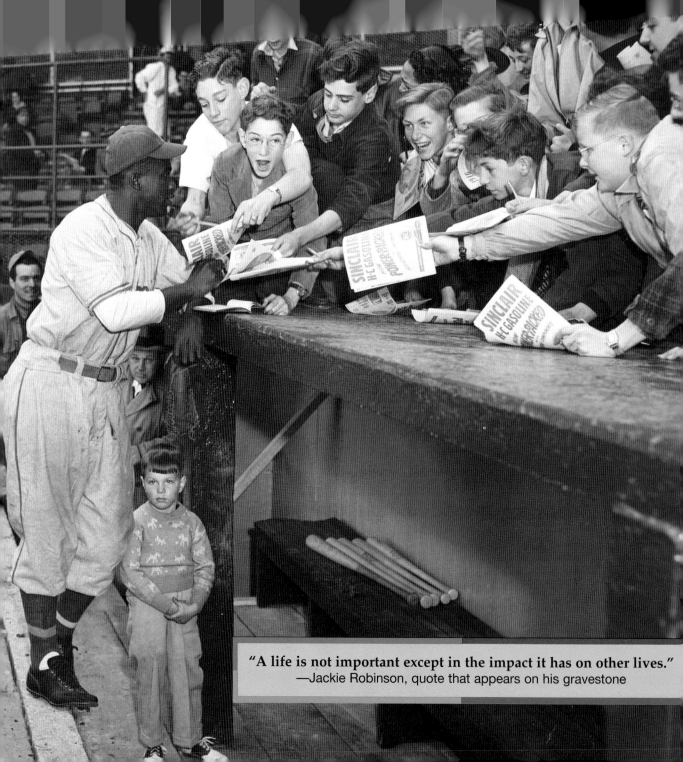

"A life is not important except in the impact it has on other lives."
—Jackie Robinson, quote that appears on his gravestone

Success

Jackie played for the Brooklyn Dodgers from 1947 until 1956. He led the Dodgers to the World Series six times. The Dodgers won the World Series in 1955.

Jackie became famous. People from all over the country came to watch him play baseball. Reporters wrote many stories about his fast base-running style. One company even started printing Jackie Robinson comics.

Jackie received many awards and honors. In 1947, he got the first Rookie of the Year award. Jackie was the first African American to appear on the cover of *Life* magazine. He was also on the cover of *Time* magazine.

Jackie starred in *The Jackie Robinson Story* in 1950. This movie was about his success as a baseball player. It was also about Jackie's work to help gain equal rights for all African Americans.

Jackie signed autographs for many fans before and after games.

"There's not an American in this country free until every one of us is free."
—Jackie Robinson

Civil Rights Leader

After Jackie retired from baseball in 1956, he worked for the National Association for the Advancement of Colored People (NAACP). This group helps African Americans gain equal rights.

Jackie helped raise money for African American causes. He helped African Americans start businesses and find places to live. Jackie opened the Jackie Robinson Construction Company in 1970. This company built houses for people who could not afford them.

Jackie worked with many civil rights leaders. He spoke at meetings with Dr. Martin Luther King Jr. Jackie often spoke for political candidates who stood up for African American rights. He also worked for the governor of New York on civil rights issues.

Jackie participated in protests for civil rights.

JACK ROOSEVELT ROBINSON

Later Years

Jackie continued to receive awards after he retired. In 1962, Jackie was the first African American elected into the National Baseball Hall of Fame.

In 1972, the Dodgers retired the number 42, Jackie's number. In 1997, every major league baseball team retired number 42. No other baseball player will ever wear Jackie's number.

Jackie died of a heart attack on October 24, 1972. He was 52 years old. After his death, Jackie received the United States' highest civilian award. President Ronald Reagan honored Jackie with the Medal of Freedom in 1984.

Jackie is remembered as a great athlete and a great civil rights leader. He broke baseball's color barrier and fought for civil rights. Jackie's courage made changes in American baseball. Jackie's courage also made changes in America.

Jackie holds his plaque at the Hall of Fame ceremony on July 22 in Cooperstown, New York.

Fast Facts about Jackie Robinson

 In 1982, Jackie became the first baseball player to appear on a U.S. postage stamp.

 Jackie's parents chose "Roosevelt" for his middle name to honor former President Theodore Roosevelt.

 The Rookie of the Year award was renamed the Jackie Robinson Award in 1987.

Dates in Jackie Robinson's Life

1919—Jackie is born on January 31 in Cairo, Georgia.

1941—Jackie becomes the first UCLA athlete honored in four sports.

1942—The U.S. Army drafts Jackie.

1945—Jackie joins the Kansas City Monarchs.

1945—The Brooklyn Dodgers sign Jackie.

1946—Rachel Isum and Jackie marry on February 10.

1947—Jackie is the first African American to break baseball's color barrier.

1947—Jackie receives the first National League Rookie of the Year award.

1949—Jackie is named the National League's Most Valuable Player.

1955—The Dodgers win the World Series Championship.

1956—Jackie retires from baseball.

1962—Jackie is elected to the National Baseball Hall of Fame.

1970—The Jackie Robinson Construction Company is formed.

1972—Jackie dies on October 24 in Stamford, Connecticut.

Words to Know

civilian (si-VIL-yuhn)—a person who is not in the military

civil rights (SIV-il RITES)—people's rights to freedom and equal treatment under the law

color barrier (KUHL-ur BA-ree-ur)—an unwritten rule that kept African Americans from joining all-white sports teams

protest (PROH-test)—a demonstration or statement against something

rookie (RUK-ee)—an athlete who is in his or her first season with a professional sports team

segregated (SEG-ruh-gay-ted)—the act of keeping people or groups apart

sharecropper (SHAIR-krop-ur)—a person who works a piece of land for food, shelter, and part of the crops grown

Read More

Abraham, Philip. *Jackie Robinson*. Real People. New York: Children's Press, 2002.

De Marco, Tony. *Jackie Robinson*. Chanhassen, Minn.: Child's World, 2002.

Gomez, Rebecca. *Jackie Robinson*. First Biographies. Edina, Minn.: Abdo, 2003.

McLeese, Don. *Jackie Robinson*. Equal Rights Leaders. Vero Beach, Fla.: Rourke, 2003.

Raatma, Lucia. *Jackie Robinson*. Compass Point Early Biographies. Minneapolis: Compass Point Books, 2001.

Useful Addresses

The Jackie Robinson Foundation
3 West 35th Street
11th Floor
New York, NY 10001-2204

National Baseball Hall of Fame
25 Main Street
P.O. Box 590
Cooperstown, NY 13326

Internet Sites

Do you want to find out more about Jackie Robinson? Let FactHound, our fact-finding hound dog, do the research for you.

Here's how:
1) Visit **http://www.facthound.com**
2) Type in the **BOOK ID** number:
   0736822240
3) Click on **FETCH IT**.

FactHound will fetch Internet sites picked by our editors just for you!

Index